# "What Every Person and Business Owner Ought to Know About Identity Theft"

*(<u>before</u> it happens)*

Copyright & Trademark Protected. All Rights Reserved.

Copyright 2016.

No part of this publication may be reproduced or transmitted in any form or by any means, mechanical or electronic, including photocopying and recording, or by any information storage and retrieval system, without permission in writing from the Author.

Published by:

Artie Bernaducci

ImportantInfo4U.com

1460 U.S. Hwy 9 N

Suite 210 A

Woodbridge, New Jersey 07095

Phone: (732) 455-9990

Toll-Free: (800) 433-3138

Email: artie@ImportantantInfo4u.com

www.ImportantInfo4U.com

Artie Bernaducci is an investment adviser representative of, and securities and advisory services are offered through, USA Financial Securities Corp. (Member FINRA/SIPC). USA Financial Securities is a registered investment adviser and is located at 6020 East Fulton Street, Ada, MI 49301. ImportantInfo4U.com and Retirement Income Advisors, LLC are not affiliated with USA Financial Securities.

"My Parents told me growing up that I could become anybody I wanted to be...so I became an Identity Thief"
(anonymous)

# Attention: Business Owners and Consumers...

## *What You Don't Know Can (and Will) Really Hurt You!*

Have you ever thought getting hacked couldn't happen to you?

Well...it could!

Your info is already OUT THERE and can be captured.

To think it can't is naïve!

There's really a world out there made up of criminals who plan every moment how to steal your, your family's and your business's information!

> That means they want your username, password and Social Security number so they can **open credit cards in your name, drain your bank accounts and seize your computer to hold it for ransom** that you'll have to pay to get back!

What can you do about it?

A LOT!

*Read this little book to get started!*

# Artie Bernaducci, Speaker & Author

Artie Bernaducci is the founder of Retirement Income Advisors, LLC, and has been working in his favorite profession since 1991. Throughout his career, his priority has been to help clients understand financial gobbledygook and make it simple for them to plan their retirement.

He quickly found effective ways to communicate so people could respond to advice and help improve their situation versus them doing nothing at all about their future. He often stated, "It was no fun to try and help someone while I used language that caused their eyes to glaze over!"

After graduating from Ball State University in Indiana with a B.S. degree in Soil Science, he was unable to find work in his major area of study, so he went into the masonry business with his family and ran his own successful company for more than a decade.

The masonry business also has its own gobbledygook, and even through a learning curve then, Artie worked hard to simplify the language in day-to-day business. With his transition to the financial world, it was a given that he apply this same approach and ensure clients could understand the industry "mumbo jumbo" in order to move for ward with planning their retirement.

Artie is passionate about helping people and enjoys connecting with his clients. His focus includes retirement and financial income planning, and especially assisting baby boomers who are approaching or are already in retirement. His aim is to educate clients and support them with the retirement knowledge they need to help them through their life stages.

He has co-authored with his colleague and friend, Denny Frasiolas, the book **"Strategies to Create Lifetime Income for Baby Boomers"**. He also speaks at seminars on retirement and financial income planning.

Artie became interested in Identity theft back in 2004 when his bank account was hacked. At the time, it was still a vague concept to him but the more he read up on the subject, the more interested he became.

Today he offers ID protection as a corollary service to his clients because he found many were without protection.

He also speaks on the subject to small businesses and professionals.

He is married to his best friend, Monica, and has 2 grown children, Rosaleen and Louis Kolydas.

His main interests are his family, bodybuilding, yoga and meditation, marketing, veganism, Oriental Medicine and "paying it forward".

# Table of Contents

SOPHISTICATION: The Changing Face of Theft In America

Just How At Risk Are You?

True ID Crime Stories

Employer BEWARE!

How Employers Can Take Precautions Against Identity Theft – And Potential Liability

Steps to TAKE

Final Words

TEST YOUR IDENTITY KNOWLEDGE

"Tiger, I think you're a victim of identity theft. There are thousands of cats with the same name as you!"

# SOPHISTICATION:

# The Changing Face of Theft in America

Every day, we face a number of dangers in America. But, while the media focuses on many of the more obvious threats, there is another that can not only be detrimental to your financial well-being, but depending on the nature of the crime, could also be a threat to your life. This is identity theft.

What exactly is identity theft? In its most broad sense, it is defined as the fraudulent acquisition of someone's private information – usually for the purpose of financial gain. But over the past few years, identity thieves have become much more sophisticated, and greedy, and are obtaining information for a number of other reasons, too.

In fact, several years ago, the most prevalent type of identity theft was what is referred to as "true name" identity theft. This is the act of stealing an individual's identity without modifying it and actually posing as the victim. But today, this type of ID theft only accounts for about 10 to 15% of overall cases.[1]

Just like most other "industries," as the Internet and other forms of communication have progressed, so have thieves' tactics for illegally obtaining information – and using it for their own personal gain, unfortunately to the detriment of millions of victims every year.

According to veteran journalist Ted Koppel, the former anchor and managing editor of ABC's "Nightline", identity theft - and cyber crime as a whole - could be devastating to the entire nation. In Koppel's book, "Lights Out", he explains how a well-designed attack on just one of the United States' three electric grids could literally cripple much of the country's infrastructure. And, in this age of cyber warfare, a laptop has become the only necessary weapon that a criminal needs.

In fact, Koppel states that several nations that are hostile towards the United States could launch such an assault at any time. Based on information from the former chief scientist of the NSA, both China and Russia have already penetrated the grid.

So, while you may have been able to protect yourself years ago with an airtight password and a great spam filter, the truth is that identity thieves are smart and savvy, and the scams today are getting harder to detect – which is why it is even more essential than ever to protect yourself before you become a victim.

In addition to just using your credit card information to make purchases, now thieves are casting a much wider net by opening cell phone accounts, obtaining drivers licenses, filing tax returns in order to obtain the refund, and even starting businesses in their victims' names.

Unfortunately, when you become a victim to this type of crime, it can affect you in a number of ways. In addition to the financial headaches that it can cause, having someone steal your very identity - in essence, become *you* - can also affect you emotionally, too.

Plus, the time that it takes to make things right again can eat into the time that you would - and should - otherwise be working, spending time with family and friends, and taking part in your other, everyday activities.

For many who have become victims of identity theft, missed work days have been a result, and in turn, job performance has suffered. And, as a result of the severe emotional distress that is typically endured, personal relationships can also oftentimes suffer.

## Today Identity theft is way more COMPLEX

Today, one of the fastest growing types of identity fraud is what is referred to as **synthetic identity theft**. This accounts for approximately 80 to 85 percent of all cases. Here, thieves will combine both real and fake information in order to create a brand new and different identity.[2]

For example, they can use your personal Social Security number and combine it with a different name, address, and phone number. Then, they can open up new bank accounts, acquire credit cards, purchase cell phones, and even buy goods and services.

While these won't actually be in your name, they will be associated with your Social Security number – and because of that, if the payments are not made, it can negatively affect your credit score and report.

Unfortunately, though, because this "fragmented" information is in someone else's name, it may take longer to reach your credit file – and because of *that*, basic fraud alerts or credit freezes typically won't help to warn you.

This also means that because it can usually take longer to find out that you've been victimized, it can also be more difficult for you to clear your name once something like this has occurred.

It usually doesn't take much for a criminal to create a brand-new identity, either. While you might think that an identity thief needs access to your entire personal file, the truth is that oftentimes all they really require is your Social

Security number or your credit card.

"If you were concerned about identity theft, you shouldn't have left your private information lying around where I could find it!"

## Just How at Risk Are *You*?

So, just how at risk are you for being a victim of identity theft?

Unfortunately, this risk may be higher than you might think.

This type of theft has been growing over time – and according to the Insurance Information Institute, in just the past six years alone, identity

thieves have stolen approximately $112 billion. Of that, $15 billion was stolen from 13.1 million U.S. consumers in 2015 alone.[4]

In addition, the way in which fraudsters have been going about this type of crime has also been branching out.

What was once a matter of swiping someone else's personal information for pure financial gain, these days **you never really know what an identity thief is going to do with your information once they have it.**

Today, it can be relatively easy for scammers to obtain your information, too - placing you at much higher risk than you might imagine. For instance, due in large part to the technological advances like the rise of mobile banking and shopping, as well as social media activity, Americans are actually at greater risk than ever before for identity theft.

In fact, because we live in such a "digital world" now, **our personal data is literally always out there.** Even seemingly "unimportant" or common information like your birth date, email address, or phone number can actually provide an ID thief all that he or she needs. This is because these items can be part of a much larger data set.

**Once an ID thief has even just a few key pieces of your information, they may be able to sell it, open new accounts in your name, or possibly even set up an entirely new life – as *you*. After this happens, it could take months, or even years, for you to realize that anything has even occurred.**

In some cases, for instance, you could then spend years unwinding a severely damaged credit report, and / or trying to recoup lost funds from your bank account. But in other cases, the legal repercussions of identity theft can be much more severe.

For example, victims can even face the risk of going to jail for crimes that they haven't committed – and oftentimes, there is absolutely no warning until it is much, much too late to prevent the situation from occurring.[5]

# TRUE IDENTITY THEFT Stories

## STORY #1

### Hey! What are you doing living in my house?

Dexter Evans has been a living nightmare for more than a dozen years now - all because someone used his Social Security number to purchase a home - and then lived in it for years!

Back in 2001, the fraudster obtained Evans's Social Security number and created his own "American Dream" by using it on a mortgage application, as well as seven additional accounts.

Over the next several years, Evans started to receive bills from Capital One and other creditors stating that he was behind on his payments - to the tune of many thousands of dollars every month. In fact, he was even denied a checking account at a local bank because the scammer already had one at another bank.

Although the fraudster has now been charged with the crime, **he currently still remains in the home that he illegally purchased with Evans' information under false pretenses.**

As for Evans, he lives in an apartment and drives an old truck because he is unable to obtain credit, and he will require the help of an attorney to straighten out his credit and his good name.

# STORY #2

## Kiddie What?

Simon Bunce, a UK resident who had his identity compromised when he used his credit card to make some online purchases from a computer in a South London restaurant.

Bunce ultimately ended up losing his six-figure job and became alienated by friends and family because his credit card was used to purchase and download child pornography.

He was later found to be innocent when investigators determined that his credit card numbers were entered into a computer in Jakarta, Indonesia at almost the same moment he was using it in London.3

The bad news for Bunce was that the major damage had already been done. With no job and his reputation in the mud, Bunce may never be able to fully recover what the identity thieves took from him.

# STORY #3

## I Know I was speeding but...

Stancy Nesby, a California single mother of four, who works two jobs to support her family. Several years ago, Nesby was pulled

over for speeding - and, while she readily admitted to driving too fast, she was arrested and taken to jail. The reason - records showed that back in 1999, she'd been busted for possession of cocaine, but had never showed up for her court appearances.

After spending three days in jail, Nesby was finally proven innocent when her fingerprints didn't match the real suspect who had used her name. The police told Nesby that they would fix the issue. But little did Nesby know, her problems were just beginning.

Two months later, she was arrested again - this time at her home. Again, when the error was discovered, officers said that they would help her to clear her name. But again, several months later, she was arrested for a third time.

In fact, over a two-year period, **Nesby was arrested or detained a total of seven times in five different jurisdictions - and one time she was hauled off right in front of her children - even though she was completely innocent.**

While this is bad enough, in other identity theft instances, you could be unable to fill your needed prescriptions for medication or have medical procedures performed, depending on how your personal information has been violated. In fact, it could literally even become a matter of life or death.

# STORY #4

## It ain't my baby!

Andery Sax received a phone call saying that her newborn baby had just tested positive for illegal drugs. The interesting thing was that

Andery hadn't given birth in years. To make matters worse, authorities showed up at her door the next day, calling her an unfit mother and threatening to take away all four of her kids.

Andery, too, was a victim of identity theft. Someone had stolen her driver's license, went to the hospital, and had a baby - leaving Andery with a $10,000 bill and a fight to clear her good name.

**But there are even bigger issues here...**

*That's because when it comes to medical ID theft, a scammer can also substitute their own information onto your medical records. This means that items like blood type, medications, and even your medical conditions can all be changed - which can essentially can become life-threatening.*

**Andery ultimately had to take a DNA test to prove that she was not the mother of the drug-addicted baby.** She still fears the long-term danger that could have been done to her medical records.

Simply keeping your computer passwords protected and your wallet secure may not always be enough to keep you safe from identity theft!

The good news is that there are ways of protecting yourself – and they can be easier and less expensive than you might think.

# EMPLOYER BEWARE!

While identity theft can cause tremendous issues for individuals, it can be an even bigger problem for employers. That's because not only is the workplace the site of so much identity theft, but also because **an employer can actually face liability if or when it occurs.**

Because companies are increasingly depending on electronic data and computer networks in order to

conduct their daily operations, growing pools of both personal and financial information are being stored and transferred online.

This can leave employees exposed to privacy violations. It can also leave both financial institutions, as well as other businesses exposed to potentially large liability if or when a breach of data security occurs.

According to Michael Hall, a certified identity risk management specialist, the workplace is the site of more than half of all ID thefts.

One reason for this is because there are several different types of identity theft – of which an employer could essentially be held liable for all.

In fact, employers could be subject to civil liability to employees whose personal information has been stolen, as well as subject to criminal liability for data theft – and, if a data breach occurs, it can also be extremely costly to a company's reputation.[6]

In the past, thieves used to care about getting money. But today, they care a whole lot more about obtaining people's information, **because they can use that to make a lot more money** – and in some cases, the individuals may or may not even realize what is happening for quite some time.

According to the FBI, more than $8 billion is lost or stolen from small businesses every year. And, based on research from the Ponemon Institute, in nearly 85% of the cases, money was stolen before the fraud was ever even detected.

In addition, while roughly 60% of businesses that suffer from business identity fraud close their doors within just one year, the effects of this type of crime to a business owner can actually go much further. That is because as a business owner, there is a great deal of personal information that is closely tied to the company. So, while this type of crime can have a substantial effect on the business, it can also destroy your personal credit and finances, too.

# Types of ID Theft That Can Occur in the Work Place

When it comes to the workplace, there are five key risks that an employer may face in terms of identity theft. This is because an employer typically

has so much personal information about their employees on file. These types of identity theft include:

- **Driver's License** – If a thief gets hold of an employee's information, they could use it to obtain a driver's license in his or her name. In turn, they could claim to be that individual in a traffic stop – or worse – resulting in that person getting their driving privileges suspended, or even revoked. **The employee could even obtain criminal charges on their driver's licenses such as DUIs – all without their knowledge.**

- **Social Security** – Even something as "harmless"

- as putting someone's Social Security number in the wrong hands can turn out to be devastating. This is because this information can be **used by someone else to get a job, and to then not pay taxes on that income.** In doing this, they – in the individual's name – would be committing a serious offense against the IRS (Internal Revenue Service).

- **Character** – If an identity thief has another individual's personal information and commits a crime, they could give the police that person's name rather than theirs. This could essentially result in **an innocent person getting arrested for the crime – not them.**

- **Medical** – With medical identity theft, a thief could use someone else's information in order to obtain health care – and, because that medical history would then include the information about someone else, **it could become life threatening if the rightful individual should later need medical care**, especially in the event of an emergency or need for surgery. Medical identity theft is actually one of the fastest growing types of identity theft today.

- **Financial** – When ID thieves get hold of a bank account and / or credit card numbers, they can quickly drain accounts and / or run up charge accounts very quickly. Not only can a victim lose money, but this **can also have an effect on his or her credit report for many years to come.**

Having personally identifiable information stolen can be extremely costly to a business. According to the Ponemon Institute, the cost for each lost record averaged $200 in 2015. This entity also found that the average overall cost to a company reached $3.8 million - and that is before considering things like loss of reputation, business partners, and consumers. (Source: Swiped: How to Protect Yourself in a World Full of

Scammers, Phishers, and Identity Thieves. By Adam Levin) So, if a company's system is breached and hundreds - or even thousands - of customers' information is compromised, this can be a financial disaster to the business.

As a business owner, though, the threat doesn't stop with just your employees' information. It can actually be much more of a threat. For example, some of the common ways in which a company can fall victim to a cyber crime include:

- Business Credit Profile - Cyber criminals can obtain and manipulate a company's Dun & Bradstreet credit information regarding the business in order to impersonate and / or defraud a company.

- Fraudulent State Business Registration - For as little as $10 or $15, a cyber-criminal can easily file a change of business address, as well as the information about the company's officers. In addition, a company that has been resolved can easily be reinstated, allowing the thief to conduct fraudulent transactions in the company's name. This can oftentimes go on for months, or even longer, without the former business owner's knowledge.

- Similar Business Name - Cyber thieves can also file a company name that is intentionally similar to another business - and in doing so, they can impersonate that company, and even deceive the company's suppliers, creditors, and financial institutions.

- False Financial Statements - By using information that is publicly available, cyber criminals can get hold of and falsify financial statements, as well as a company's annual report, in order to obtain business loans and lines of credit.

- Virtual Office or Phone Service - Today, may businesses will lease "virtual" office space, which can allow them to use a verifiable physical office location, as well as a mailing address. But, thieves can also do the very same thing in order to impersonate a company. Likewise, companies that use VoIP (Voice over IP telephone service that utilizes the Internet) can also be at risk by criminals that can establish a phone number that appears to be a company's local number or landline.

- Fake Company Website - Today, a website can be established in just a matter of a few hours, or even less. Cyber criminals can easily create a website in the name of another company - which even includes third party logos such as the Better Business Bureau and Verisign - in order to impersonate a legitimate company. (Source: http://www.idefendbusiness.com/how_it_happens.aspx)

- Viruses - Cyber criminals can also infect a company's computer network with viruses - many of which can lay dormant for a period of time. Then, at an appointed time, or when given a specific command, the virus can essentially become a platform for launching an attack themselves. For instance, a company's network could be infected with a Trojan horse software that turns into a platform for launching a distributed denial of service attack. With this type of an attack, an Internet resource is targeted with innumerable requests, which will then make it completely unavailable and can cause a significant disruption for the affected business. In some cases, this type of an attack could even result in the victim company being liable for spreading malicious code, causing disruptions in service that could entail further liability - or worse. For example, if a company that has an online store is infected with a virus, and the people who make purchases from the company's website end up getting infected with a virus as a result, the company could actually be liable for damages. (Source: Cyber Insurance 2015: Guide for Small and Medium Businesses)

Any company, large or small, can be at risk of a cyber attack - even those that may have put some precautions in place. For example, in May 2014, the online auction website eBay announced that it was the victim of an attack. This hack resulted in 233 million users having their personal information stolen.

According to Forbes, the attack was launched between February and March of that year. Among the information stolen was the username and passwords of hundreds of millions of users, as well as their addresses and phone numbers.

Smaller companies may even be more at risk than large corporations. This is because cyber criminals are aware that most small businesses are not adequately protected. For instance, a small medical clinic that has been in business for many years may have medical information stored on their servers for hundreds, or even thousands, of its clients. But even if a company doesn't handle sensitive data like medical records, it can still have the physical addresses, credit card numbers, and / or banking information of its customers.

In addition to a lack of protection, small businesses may also be more at risk to a cyber attack because in many instances, the company may be using older computer equipment that is not as secure, older software that could be more vulnerable, and / or an IT department that may not be fully trained in dealing with the most current types of cyber threats. Further, the increased reliance of small businesses on "the cloud" in order to store information can also put the company at more risk of a data breach.

In today's world, it is literally impossible to overestimate the threat that is posed to businesses by hackers who have the motivation and the skills to penetrate systems, steal data, and even cause technological and economic disruption.

## How Does Identity Theft Occur in the Workplace?

There are a number of ways in which identity theft can occur in the workplace. And, while we may often hear about large corporations being "hacked," resulting in employees' and customers' information being compromised, thieves don't necessarily always target just the largest companies with the biggest databases.

In fact, identity theft really isn't so much a "computer" or a data issue, as it is a people issue. For example, some of the primary causes of information breaches in the workplace can include the following:

- Dishonest employees
- Disgruntled employees
- Careless and / or untrained employees

- Lost or stolen laptops
- Hackers
- Service providers
- Contractors
- Visitors

It is important to note that the threat to sensitive information to a company doesn't necessarily originate outside of the business from a large technical criminal entity. In fact, one of the most common ways in which data is stolen from companies is via a USB drive, or other portable storage device, that can take data directly off of the company's computers. Even something as unsuspecting as an Mp3 player can have a large amount of storage space and can carry out this type of crime.

So, if an untrustworthy employee, outside contractor, or anyone else who has access to the company's physical computers decides to lift the information, they could easily download sensitive data, and in turn, potentially expose the company to a substantial amount of liability.

Oftentimes, these aren't small, petty crimes, either. In

fact, as cyber criminals become more sophisticated, the crimes are getting larger, as are the "profits" for the criminals. In many cases, being unprepared can leave a company or a business owner holding the proverbial financial bag.

As an example, the owner of Seagate Foods, the company that operates Captain D's seafood restaurants, notified authorities that someone had apparently gotten hold of the company's taxpayer identification number. In doing so, the thieves created more than 100 fake W-2 forms and in turn, reported more than $4 million in non-existent salaries to state and federal agencies. This was most likely a scheme with the intention of collecting fraudulent tax refunds. When all was said and done, Seagate was left owning more than $800,000 in payroll taxes.

This isn't an isolated incident. In fact, according to the IRS National Taxpayer Advocate, since 2008, tax-related identity theft has increased by 650%. One reason for this is because a company's EIN (federal employer identification number) is, in many ways, like a Social Security number for businesses. This number is required for numerous transactions that companies engage in regularly, including opening business bank accounts, obtaining business loans and credit accounts, merchant credit card processing, and state and federal tax filing.

There are many different types of fraudulent accounts that can be opened by cyber criminals with just a company's name, address, and EIN number.

Not all cyber criminals are highly knowledgeable computer "techies," either. Law enforcement officials state that today, gang members are increasingly focusing on these types of crimes, primarily because they are safer and more lucrative than selling drugs as a source of income. In fact, Detective Craig Catlin of the North Miami Beach Police Department Gang Unit has gone so far as to call it an "epidemic" among the city's street gangs. As he states, "Why sling dope on the corner of an apartment building, when you can rent a room at a hotel nearby and have a tax return party? You can make up to $40,000 or $50,000 in one night." (Source:http://www.businessidtheft.org/Education/BusinessIDTheftScams/BusinessEINandTaxFraud)

# How Employers Can Take Precautions Against Identity Theft – And Potential Liability

With so many ways in which information can be compromised in the workplace, what can companies do to help safeguard their employees from identity theft – and themselves against potential liability?

There are several potential solutions, starting with making the security of information a priority. **In fact, today, there are several federal and state laws and regulations that concern information privacy and security, including the Gramm-Leach-Bliley Act for financial information, and the Health Insurance Portability and Accountability Act for health information.**

Ensuring that information is protected in the best manner possible will usually begin with having a

well-designed plan. Within that plan should include set training procedures for employees, as well as protocol for signing an agreement to follow information security standards.

If a company does outsource any of its functions to outside contractors, it is absolutely essential to thoroughly investigate that company – especially if the contractor will have access to internal data or information.

Over the past decade, it is estimated that more than a billion sensitive records with personally identifiable information have been leaked. That information is most likely in the hands of several different criminal enterprises that have bought and sold it multiple times. Even if this information is not unified or organized, cyber criminals still have the ability to piece it together in order to create usable blocks of re-identified information that can be used in the commission of fraud. (Source: Swiped: How to Protect Yourself in a World Full of Scammers, Phishers, and Identity Thieves)

**In terms of both employee protection and company liability, it can be key to offer identity theft protection as an employee benefit. Just as the company would provide any other type of**

**insurance protection, ID theft protection can provide insurance coverage in the case of an identity theft situation.**

**For a small monthly premium, the employee could obtain Identity protection, as well as other important services. In this case, the plan should ideally include restoration services that could assist the employee in reclaiming their identity.**

**It is also essential to consider business owner coverage for identity theft. This is because consumer identity theft protection services do not provide help for business ID fraud. Also, while your business**

liability policy may offer some amount of protection, at best this is usually minimal.

With that in mind, business owners should take a close look at their Commercial General Liability policy, as well as any Errors & Omissions coverage that they may have in order to determine what, if any, protection they may have. Many business owners may think that they are covered when in reality, they are not.

One of the key advantages to having business owner protection is that it can not only provide the company with business identity monitoring

and financial reimbursement, but many of these options today will also provide coverage for sending in a response team to help with mitigating the damage. This can be crucial if a business becomes the victim of a cyber attack.

This type of coverage can also provide a business owner with identity fraud resources, such as guidelines that business owners should know in order to help preventing the company from being targeted. By using proactive measures to help in preventing an event from ever occurring, a business owner can save a tremendous amount of money.

# STEPS TO TAKE...

Identity theft is a serious and growing issue today – and because of that, consumers need to protect themselves from scammers that can be extremely savvy.

Because there is so much interconnection in the world today, it is not always easy to determine where a cyber attack might come from, when it might occur, or why. But in many cases, it isn't necessarily a question of IF, but WHEN an attack may occur. Oftentimes, the only real defense a consumer or a business has is to have adequate procedures and technology in place to reduce the chances of the attack being successful and to mitigate the fallout if it does occur.

The good news is that you can do things to help ensure that you are better protected from this issue.

*Minimizing Your Exposure*

Minimizing your exposure is one of the best ways that you can protect yourself from identity thieves.

Today, with so much information being transferred back and forth online, it is essential that you **use caution with even the most basic of details.**

With that in mind, practice caution if you receive an email that requests personal or sensitive information. Prior to providing any personal or financial details, ensure that the source is reputable and authentic. One of the best ways to do so is to find the correct contact information and call them back directly.

It is also important to protect yourself in other ways, too, such as:

- Properly storing passwords (and changing them regularly)
- Not sharing too much information via social media
- Properly storing documents
- Freezing your credit
- Using security software on your computer (and keeping it up to date)
- Not carrying unneeded personal information with you when you go out
- Not leaving personal items unsecured in a vehicle or other area where it could be compromised

## Monitoring Your Accounts

It is also wise to regularly monitor your financial accounts. This includes regularly checking your credit score and report for any sudden changes.

Every year, consumers are allowed to obtain a free copy of their credit report by visiting www.annualcreditreport.com. Be sure to read over your report carefully - and if there are any errors on it, contact the credit reporting agency immediately in writing and request to have them fixed.

You should also check on your major accounts on a daily basis in order to ensure that they are all in-tact. This includes your bank accounts (savings and checking), as well as any investment accounts that you may have.

# What to Do If You Become a Victim

If you are unable to avoid becoming a victim of identity theft, it is absolutely essential that you act on it immediately. There are a couple of different avenues that you can take in dealing with the issue.

First, you could take on the fraudsters yourself by setting up alerts via all of the credit reporting agencies, as well as working with your bank, credit cards, and other areas that have been affected.

Or, you could alternatively enroll in a program that does some or all of the work for you. Going with this option can save you a tremendous amount of time, along with taking care of additional tasks and monitoring that you may not be able to do on your own.

In most cases, the cost is minimal - especially in return for the money and time that it can ultimately end up saving you.

# FINAL WORDS...

If you think that you're prepared for anything that life can throw your way – you may need to think again. It only takes a second for a scammer to get ahold of your personal information and to in turn, ruin your financial life – and your identity. I can help you with putting together the strategies that you need to ensure that you and your identity are safe.

Remember, a good offense is always the best defense. Although identity theft can be devastating, there are ways that you can protect yourself from these types of predators. Just like the old saying goes, "an ounce of prevention is worth a pound of cure." Except in this case, it could be worth much, much more.

So, if you haven't protected yourself yet, WHY NOT and what might it cost if you become a victim of Identity Theft? Remember the stories you read in the preceding pages. It is NOT just financial!

Protect yourself now and you just may save yourself many hours of anguish and perhaps many thousands of dollars!

Take the next step right now:

## VISIT:
www.ImportantInfo4U.com

## EMAIL:
artie@ImportantInfo4U.com

## CALL: (732) 455-9990

# TEST YOUR IDENTITY THEFT KNOWLEDGE

## IDENTITY THEFT QUIZ

*Identity Theft Quiz: A Quiz for Consumers*

Identity thieves use many ways of getting your personal financial information so they can make fraudulent charges or withdrawals from your accounts. Do you know how you can reduce the risk of becoming a victim of identity theft? Take this simple quiz, and see how you score:

1. **When I keep my ATM cards and credit cards in my wallet, I never write my PIN (Personal Identification Number) on any of my cards.**

**Reason:** *If you lose your ATM or credit card, identity thieves or other criminals can have instant access to your bank or credit-card account.*

2. **When I leave my house, I take with me only the ATM and credit cards I need for personal or business purchases.**

**Reason:** *If your wallet or purse is lost or stolen, and you're carrying fewer cards, you'll have to make fewer calls to banks and credit-card companies to report the losses, and the odds of fraudulent charges in your name will be lower.*

3. **When I get my monthly credit-card bills, I always look carefully at the specific transactions charged to my account before I pay the bill.**

**Reason:** *Someone who gets your credit-card number and expiration date doesn't need the actual card to charge purchases to your account. If you don't look closely at your credit-card statement each month, you might not have any recourse if fraudulent transactions go through and you don't dispute them promptly with your credit-card company. As soon as you see unauthorized charges on your statement, contact the credit-card company immediately to report them.*

**4. When I get my monthly bank statements, credit-card bills, or other documents with personal financial information on them, I always shred them before putting them in the trash.**

**Reason:** *Some identity thieves aren't shy about "dumpster diving" - literally climbing into dumpsters or rooting through trash bins to look for identifying information that someone threw out. Buying and using a shredder on your home or office is an inexpensive way to frustrate dumpster divers and protect your personal data.*

**5. When I get mail saying I've been preapproved for a credit card, and don't want to accept or activate that card, I always tear up or shred the preapproval forms before putting them in the trash.**

**Reason:** *If you throw out the documents without tearing them up or shredding them, "dumpster divers" can send them back to the credit-card company, pretending to be you but saying that your address has changed. If they can use the account from a new location, you may not know the account's being used in your name until you see it on a credit report (see below).*

**6. I request a copy of my credit report at least once a year.**

**Reason:** *Any consumer can request one free copy of his or her credit report per year. Reviewing your credit report can help you find out if someone has opened unauthorized financial accounts, or taken out unauthorized loans, in your name. Contact the three* major credit bureaus - Equifax (1-800-685-1111), Experian (1-888-397-3742), or Trans Union (1-800-916-8800) - to request a copy.

**7. If the volume of the mail I get at home has dropped off substantially, I always check with my local post office to see if anyone has improperly filed a change-of-address card in my name.**

**Reason:** *Some identity thieves may try to take over your credit card and bank accounts, and delay your discovery of their criminal activities, by having your mail diverted to a new address where they can go through it without your knowledge. Your local post office should have on file any change-of-address cards, and can respond if you find that someone is improperly diverting your mail.*

**8. If I think that I may be a victim of identity theft, I immediately contact:**

The Federal Trade Commission to report the situation and get guidance on how to deal with it.

The three major credit bureaus to inform them of the situation.

My local police department to have an officer take a report.

Any businesses where the identity thief fraudulently conducted transactions in my name.

**Reason:** *Identity theft is a crime under federal law, and under the laws of more than 44 states, that carries serious penalties including imprisonment and fines. To help law enforcement in investigating and prosecuting identity theft, the Federal Trade Commission (FTC) maintains a national database of complaints by identity theft victims.*

The FTC, through a toll-free hotline (1-877-ID-THEFT), can also help you decide what steps to take in trying to remedy the situation and restore your good name and credit. Credit bureaus should also be notified so that they can flag your credit report. Local police, by taking a report and providing you with a copy, can help you show creditors that an identity thief has been conducting certain transactions in your name and without your permission.

## How did you do on this quiz? If you said even 2 or 3 "NO's", it means that you need to take more of the precautions described in this quiz and book.

Remember that identity thieves, unlike robbers or fraudsters, don't have to have any personal contact with you in order to commit their crimes.

The more you do to protect your personal information, the lower the odds that you'll become a victim of identity theft.

# Sources

1. The Changing Face of Identity Theft. Identity Theft America. (https://www.ftc.gov/sites/default/files/documents/public_comments/credit-report-freezes-534030-00033/534030-00033.pdf)

2. Ibid.

3. 3 Identity Theft Horror Stories That Will Make your Toes Curl. (http://www.dumblittleman.com/2013/10/3-identity-theft-horror-stories-that.html)

4. Insurance Information Institute. (http://www.iii.org/fact-statistic/identity-theft-and-cybercrime)

5. A Scheme You've Never Heart of Might Ruin Your Summer. Yahoo Finance. June 17, 2016.

6. Employers Face Liability for Five Kinds of Identity Theft. Society for Human Resource Management.